AMPHIBIANS

GRAHAM MEADOWS & CLAIRE VIAL

Contents

Dominie Press, Inc.

About Amphibians

Amphibians are one of the five main groups of **vertebrates.**

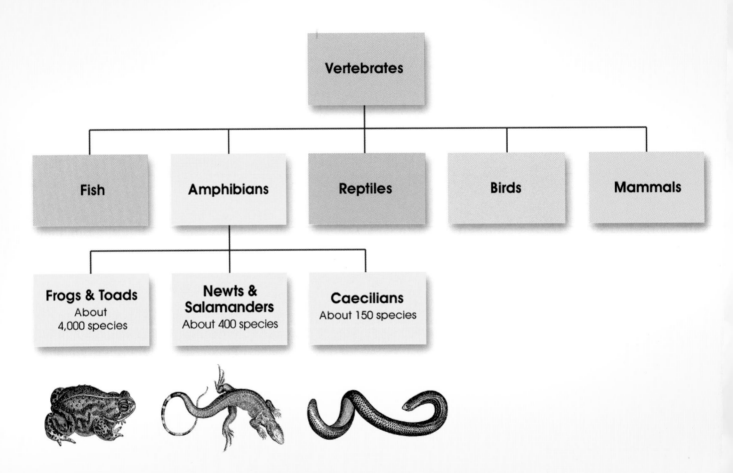

There are nearly five thousand **species** of amphibians.

There are five key features of amphibians:

* They are cool-blooded—that means their body temperature is similar to that of their surroundings.

* They need a moist **environment**.

* Their skin is usually soft and moist, and it has no scales, hair, or feathers.

* Most species of amphibians live part of their lives on land, and part of their lives in fresh water.

* Their eggs do not have a waterproof shell. They must be laid in water so that they do not dry out.

 The study of amphibians and reptiles is called herpetology.

MILLIONS OF YEARS AGO

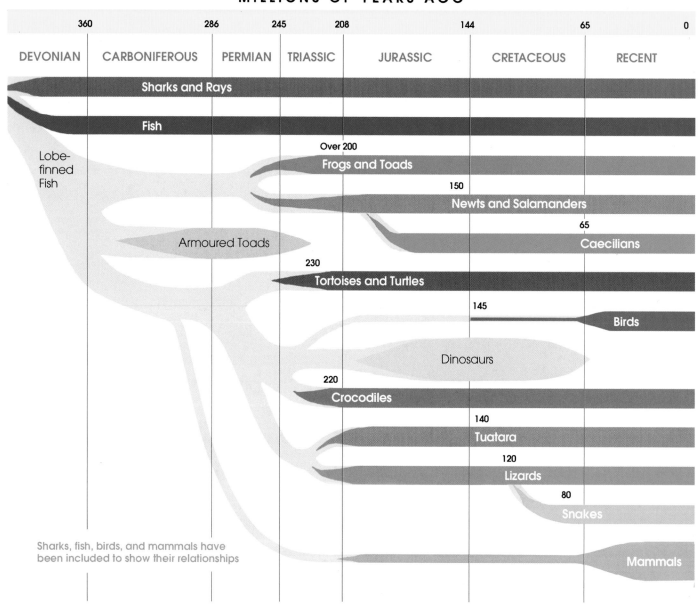

| 360 | 286 | 245 | 208 | 144 | 65 | 0 |

DEVONIAN | CARBONIFEROUS | PERMIAN | TRIASSIC | JURASSIC | CRETACEOUS | RECENT

Sharks and Rays

Fish

Lobe-finned Fish

Over 200

Frogs and Toads

150

Newts and Salamanders

65

Caecilians

Armoured Toads

230

Tortoises and Turtles

145

Birds

Dinosaurs

220

Crocodiles

140

Tuatara

120

Lizards

80

Snakes

Sharks, fish, birds, and mammals have
been included to show their relationships

Mammals

How Amphibians Evolved

Based on their study of **fossils,** scientists believe the **evolution** of amphibians began more than 360 million years ago. This time period was called the Devonian Period. During this period forests first appeared, and **primitive** fish became plentiful.

The earliest amphibians looked very much like fish, and they probably spent their entire lives in water. Over a period of many millions of years, some amphibian species became adapted to living part of their lives on land.

 Amphibians evolved later than fish, but earlier than reptiles.

How They Got Their Name

The word *amphibian* comes from the Greek word *amphibios,* which means "living a double life." Amphibians were given their name because many of them, such as the golden bell frog, live the early part of their lives in water. They spend some or all of their adult lives on land.

Golden Bell Frog

African Clawed Frog

Not all amphibians lead a "double life." Some species, such as the African clawed frog, spend their adult lives in water.

Types of Amphibians

Scientists classify amphibians into three groups called **orders**.

Order 1—Frogs and Toads

Adult frogs and toads, such as the cane toad, have large eyes and squat bodies. They have four legs. Their back legs, which are long and powerful, are used for jumping and hopping. They have no tails.

Cane Toad

Fire Salamander

Order 2—Salamanders and Newts

Like most species of salamanders and newts, adult fire salamanders have four legs of roughly equal size. They also have tails.

 One primitive species of frog has what looks like a short tail, but it is not an actual tail. This species is called the tailed frog.

Order 3—Caecilians

Caecilians have no legs. Most of them do not have tails. They have long bodies and smooth skin. Many of them look like eels or worms. They live only in moist, **tropical** areas. Most caecilian species spend much of their lives burrowed under the ground.

One species of caecilian that is found in South America lives all of its life in water. Known as a rubber eel or a black eel, it is commonly kept as a pet in home aquariums.

The largest caecilian measures about four feet in length. The smallest is just over four inches long.

◀ *Caecilian*

Where Amphibians Live

Frogs and toads live in most parts of the world. The greatest numbers of frogs and toads are found in humid, tropical environments.

Most salamanders are found in the **northern hemisphere**, especially in cool, moist forests. Some salamanders live in humid tropical areas in Mexico, Central America, and the northwestern area of South America.

◀ *Golden Bell Frog*

Red Salamander

 Amphibians do not live in Antarctica, the Arctic, or in extremely hot deserts because their moist skin would either freeze or dry out.

How They Stay Moist

Amphibians do not have shells, scales, hair, or feathers that would help prevent the loss of water through their skin. To prevent their bodies from drying out, amphibians that live on land stay in wet environments. As an additional protection, they have special skin glands that keep their skin moist. Some amphibians also have glands in their skin that give out poisonous substances. One example of this type of amphibian is the poison arrow frog.

Poison Arrow Frog

Cane Toad

A toad's skin is thicker and drier than that of other amphibians. This type of skin enables toads like the cane toad to live in hot, dry environments.

Their Skin

An amphibian's skin can absorb water. In fact, many species of amphibians don't need to drink at all. They can absorb all the water they need through their skin.

Common Frog

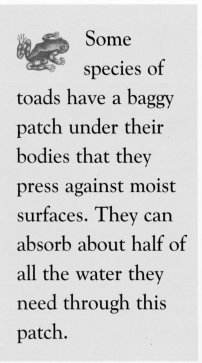 Some species of toads have a baggy patch under their bodies that they press against moist surfaces. They can absorb about half of all the water they need through this patch.

Red-bellied Newt

Frogs and other amphibians can breathe through their skin by taking in oxygen from the air and water. Most adult amphibians also have lungs to help them breathe. They can also breathe through the soft skin of their mouth and throat.

Some amphibians, such as newts, spend most of their adult lives under water. They usually breathe through their skin, but sometimes they come to the water's surface to take a breath of air.

Their Body Temperature

Amphibians are cool-blooded, which means their body temperature varies with changes in the temperature of their environment. Tree frogs and other amphibians rely on heat from the sun to warm them up, and shade to cool them down. This helps them keep their body at a temperature that is slightly higher than the temperature of their environment.

◀ *Tree Frog*

To survive very cold conditions, amphibians enter a **dormant** stage called hibernation. During hibernation, they stay under ground or deep enough under water to avoid being frozen in ice.

 Amphibians can raise their body temperature by sitting in the sun or lying on warm rocks.

◀ *Dormant Frog*

Their Diet

Some amphibian **larvae**, such as tadpoles, **graze** on plants and algae. Salamander larvae eat small **invertebrates**. Adult amphibians, such as the golden bell frog, are **carnivores** that eat a wide variety of food. Their **diet** consists mainly of invertebrates, especially insects. Large frogs, toads, and salamanders also catch and eat small reptiles, birds, and mammals.

Salamanders living on land, and certain species of frogs, use their long, sticky tongues to catch their prey.

 Some amphibians hunt for their food. Other amphibians just sit and wait for their food to come to them.

Golden Bell Frog ▶

Their Life Cycles

After a young amphibian hatches from an egg into a larva—and before it becomes an adult—it goes through major changes in its body shape and structure. These changes are called **metamorphosis**.

The larva of a frog, which is called a tadpole,

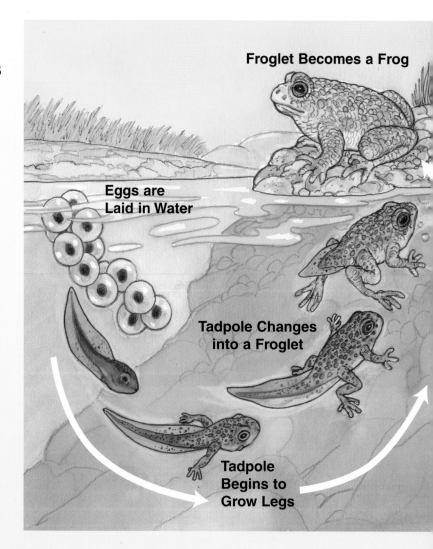

Froglet Becomes a Frog

Eggs are Laid in Water

Tadpole Changes into a Froglet

Tadpole Begins to Grow Legs

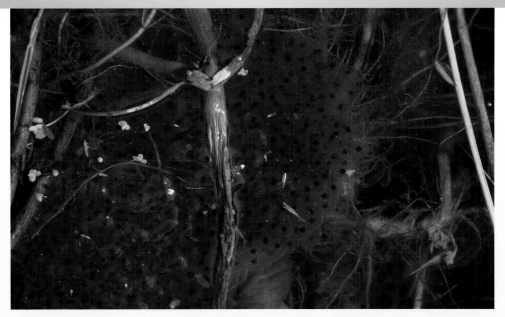

*Amphibian eggs do not have a shell. They are **gelatinous**.*

grows legs as its tail gradually gets shorter and finally disappears. Eventually the tadpole changes into a froglet, which then grows into an adult frog. This is an example of metamorphosis.

 The word *metamorphosis* comes from two Greek words: *meta*, meaning *change*, and *morpho*, meaning *form*.

Glossary

carnivores:	Animals that hunt, catch, and eat other animals
diet:	The food that an animal or a person usually eats
dormant:	Inactive; sleeping
environment:	Setting; surroundings
evolution:	Natural, gradual development
fossils:	Preserved remains of an animal or a plant
gelatinous:	Not solid; resembling jelly
graze:	To eat, or feed on plants
invertebrates:	Animals that do not have a backbone
larvae:	Immature, early-stage forms of animals
metamorphosis:	A series of natural changes in physical form
northern hemisphere:	The half of the Earth located north of the equator
orders:	Related families of organisms
primitive:	Ancient; prehistoric
species:	Types of animals that have something in common
tropical:	Areas that are very warm throughout the year
vertebrates:	Animals that have a spinal column and a well-developed brain

Index